Book Two

Christopher Columbus • Autumn Harvest • The Weather

Draw · Write · NOW®

by
Marie Hablitzel
and
Kim Stitzer

*A Drawing
and Handwriting
Course for Kids!*

Barker Creek Publishing, Inc. • Poulsbo, Washington

Dedicated to...

...my grandchildren.
I have enjoyed drawing with you! — M.H.

...Michelle's teachers — Kayte Ruggieri-Vande Putte and Maureen Todd. — K.S.

The text on the handwriting pages is set in a custom
font created from Marie Hablitzel's handwriting.
The drawings are done using Prismacolor pencils
outlined with a black PaperMate FLAIR!® felt tip pen.

BARKER CREEK

Published by Barker Creek Publishing, Inc.
P.O. Box 2610 • Poulsbo, WA 98370-2610
800•692•5833 FAX: 360•613•2542
barkercreek.com

Text and Illustration Copyright © 1995 by Kim Hablitzel Stitzer

Book layout by Judy Richardson
Printed in Hong Kong

Library of Congress Catalog Card Number: 93-73893
Publisher's Cataloging in Publication Data:
Hablitzel, Marie, 1920 - 2007
Draw•Write•Now®, Book Two : A drawing and handwriting course for kids!
(second in series)

Summary: A collection of drawing and handwriting lessons for children. *Book Two* focuses on Christopher Columbus, harvest time and the weather. Second book in the *Draw•Write•Now®* series.

1. Drawing — Technique — Juvenile Literature. 2. Drawing — Study and Teaching (Elementary). 3. Penmanship.
4. Columbus, Christopher — Juvenile Literature. 5. Autumn. 6. Weather — Juvenile Literature.
I. Stitzer, Kim, 1956 -   , coauthor. II. Title.
741.2   [372.6]

ISBN: 978-0-9639307-2-9

Eighteenth Printing

About this book...

For most children, drawing is their first form of written communication. Long before they master the alphabet and sentence syntax, children express themselves creatively on paper through line and color.

As children mature, their imaginations often race ahead of their drawing skills. By teaching them to see complex objects as combinations of simple shapes and encouraging them to develop their fine-motor skills through regular practice, they can better record the images they see so clearly in their minds.

This book contains a collection of beginning drawing lessons and text for practicing handwriting. These lessons were developed by a teacher who saw her second-grade students becoming increasingly frustrated with their drawing efforts and disenchanted with repetitive handwriting drills.

For more than 30 years, Marie Hablitzel refined what eventually became a daily drawing and handwriting curriculum. Marie's premise was simple —drawing and handwriting require many of the same skills. And, regular practice in a supportive environment is the key to helping children develop

Coauthors Marie Hablitzel (left)
and her daughter, Kim Stitzer

their technical skills, self-confidence and creativity. As a classroom teacher, Marie intertwined her daily drawing and handwriting lessons with math, science, social studies, geography, reading and creative writing. She wove an educational tapestry that hundreds of children have found challenging, motivating — and fun!

Although Marie is now retired, her drawing and handwriting lessons continue to be used in the classroom. With the assistance of her daughter, Kim Stitzer, Marie shares more than 150 of her lessons in the eight-volume *Draw•Write•Now®* series.

In *Draw•Write•Now®, Book One,* children explore life on a farm, kids and critters and storybook characters. *Books Two* through *Six* feature topics as diverse as Christopher Columbus, the weather, Native Americans, the polar regions, young Abraham Lincoln, beaver ponds and life in the sea. In *Draw•Write•Now®, Books Seven and Eight,* children circle the globe while learning about animals of the world.

We hope your children and students enjoy these lessons as much as ours have!

—*Carolyn Hurst, Publisher*

Look for these books in the *Draw•Write•Now,* series...

Book One: On the Farm, Kids and Critters, Storybook Characters
Book Two: Christopher Columbus, Autumn Harvest, The Weather
Book Three: Native Americans, North America, The Pilgrims
Book Four: The Polar Regions, The Arctic, The Antarctic
Book Five: The United States, From Sea to Sea, Moving Forward
Book Six: Animals & Habitats: On Land, Ponds and Rivers, Oceans
Book Seven: Animals of the World, Part I: Forest Animals
Book Eight: Animals of the World, Part II: Grassland and Desert Animals

For additional information call 1-800-692-5833
or visit barkercreek.com

Table of Contents

A table of contents is like a map. It guides you to the places you want to visit in a book. Pick a subject you want to draw, then turn to the page listed beside the picture.

For more information on the *Draw•Write•Now*® series, see page 3. For suggestions on how to use this book, see page 6. For a review of handwriting tips, see page 8.

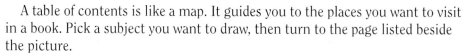
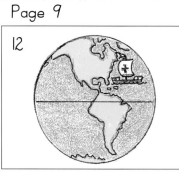 

 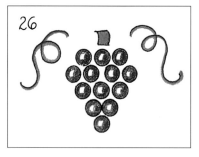 

A few tips to get started...

This is a book for children and their parents, teachers and caregivers. Although most young people can complete the lessons in this book quite successfully on their own, a little help and encouragement from a caring adult can go a long way toward building a child's self-confidence, creativity and technical skills.

Busy Beavers by Natalie Perry, age 8
from Draw•Write•Now®, Book Six

The following outline contains insights from the 30-plus years the authors have worked with the material in this book. Realizing that no two children or classrooms are alike, the authors encourage you to modify these lessons to best suit the needs of your child or classroom. Each **Draw•Write•Now®** lesson includes five parts:

1. Introduce the subject.
2. Draw the subject.
3. Draw the background.
4. Practice handwriting.
5. Color the drawing.

As presented here, each child will need a pencil, an eraser, drawing paper, penmanship paper and either crayons, color pencils or felt tip markers to complete a lesson.

1. Introduce the Subject

Begin the lesson by generating interest in the subject with a story, discussion, poem, photograph or song. The questions on the illustrated notes scattered throughout this book are examples of how interest can be built along a related theme. Answers to these questions and the titles of several theme-related books are on pages 22, 48 and 62.

2. Draw the Subject

Have the children draw with a pencil. Encourage them to draw lightly because some lines (shown as dashed lines on the drawing lessons) will need to be erased. Point out the shapes and lines in the subject as the children work through the lesson. Help the children see that complex objects can be viewed as combinations of lines and simple shapes.

Help the children be successful! Show them how to position the first step on their papers in an appropriate size. Initially, the children may find some shapes difficult to draw. If they do, provide a pattern for them to trace, or draw the first step for them. Once they fine-tune their skills and build their self-confidence, their ability and creativity will take over. For lesson-specific drawing tips and suggestions, refer to *Teaching Tips* on pages 63–64.

3. Draw the Background

Encourage the children to express their creativity and imagination in the backgrounds they add to their pictures. Add to their creative libraries by demonstrating various ways to draw trees, horizons and other details. Point out background details in the drawings in this book, illustrations from other books, photographs and works of art.

Encourage the children to draw their world by looking for basic shapes and lines in the things they see around them. Ask them to draw from their imaginations by using their developing skills. For additional ideas on motivating children to draw creatively, see pages 20–21, 46–47 and 60–61.

4. Practice Handwriting

In place of drills — rows of e's, r's and so on — it is often useful and more motivating to have children write complete sentences when practicing their handwriting. When the focus is on handwriting — rather than spelling or vocabulary enrichment — use simple words that the children can easily read and spell. Begin by writing each word with the children, demonstrating how individual letters are formed and stressing proper spacing. Start slowly. One or two sentences may be challenging enough in the beginning. Once the children are consistently forming their letters correctly, encourage them to work at their own pace.

There are many ways to adapt these lessons for use with your child or classroom. For example, you may want to replace the authors' text with your own words. You may want to let the children compose sentences to describe their drawings or answer the theme-related questions found throughout the book. You may prefer to replace the block alphabet used in this book with a cursive, D'Nealian® or other alphabet style. If you are unfamiliar with the various alphabet styles used for teaching handwriting, consult your local library. A local elementary school may also be able to recommend an appropriate alphabet style and related resource materials.

Pueblo Village by Ali Garrett, age 7
from Draw•Write•Now®, Book Three

5. Color the Picture

Children enjoy coloring their own drawings. The beautiful colors, however, often cover the details they have so carefully drawn in pencil. To preserve their efforts, you may want to have the children trace their pencil lines with black crayons or fine-tipped felt markers.

Crayons—When coloring with crayons, have the children outline their drawings with a black crayon *after* they have colored their pictures (the black crayon may smear if they do their outlining first).

Columbus's Ship by Evan Perry, age 6
from Draw•Write•Now®, Book Two

Color Pencils—When coloring with color pencils, have the children outline their drawings with a felt tip marker *before* they color their drawings.

Felt Tip Markers—When coloring with felt tip markers, have the children outline their drawings with a black marker *after* they have colored their pictures.

Your comments are appreciated!
How are you sharing Draw•Write•Now® with your children or students? The authors would appreciate hearing from you. Write to Marie Hablitzel and Kim Stitzer, c/o Barker Creek Publishing, Inc., P.O. Box 2610, Poulsbo, WA 98370, USA or visit our Web site at www.barkercreek.com.

Grizzly Bear by Brady Flynn, age 7
from Draw•Write•Now®, Book Eight

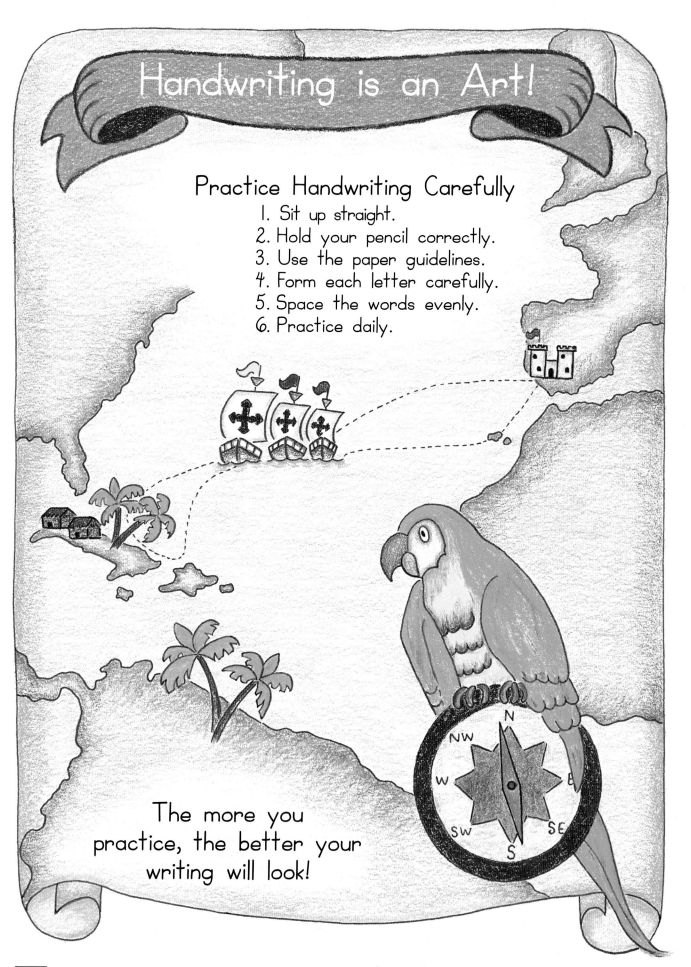

Handwriting is an Art!

Practice Handwriting Carefully
1. Sit up straight.
2. Hold your pencil correctly.
3. Use the paper guidelines.
4. Form each letter carefully.
5. Space the words evenly.
6. Practice daily.

The more you practice, the better your writing will look!

Christopher Columbus

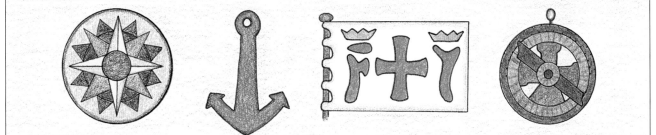

Columbus lived by the sea.
Sailors told him stories.
He read books on sailing.
He studied maps.

When did Columbus live?

Columbus

Question answered on page 22

1.

2.

3.

4.

5.

6.

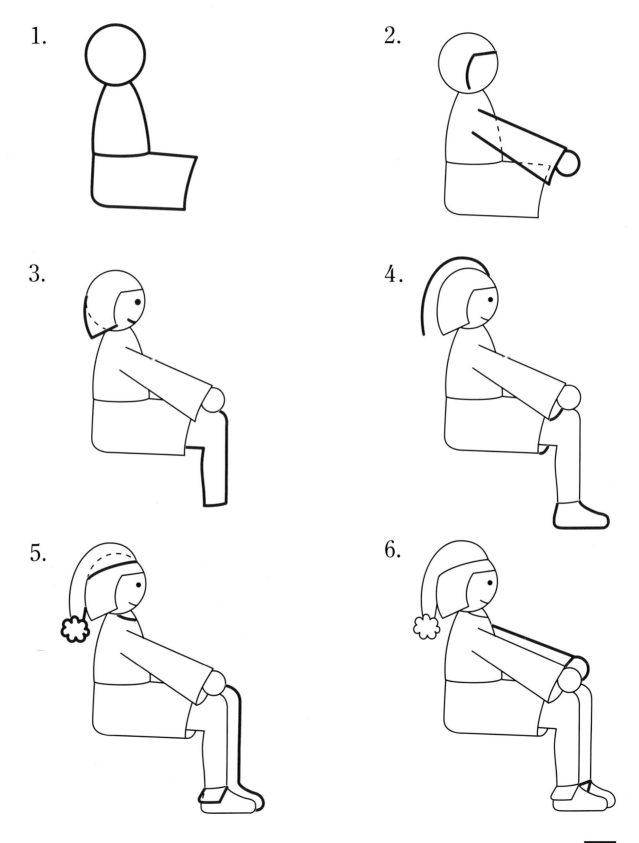

Sailing West

Teaching Tip on page 64
Question answered on page 22

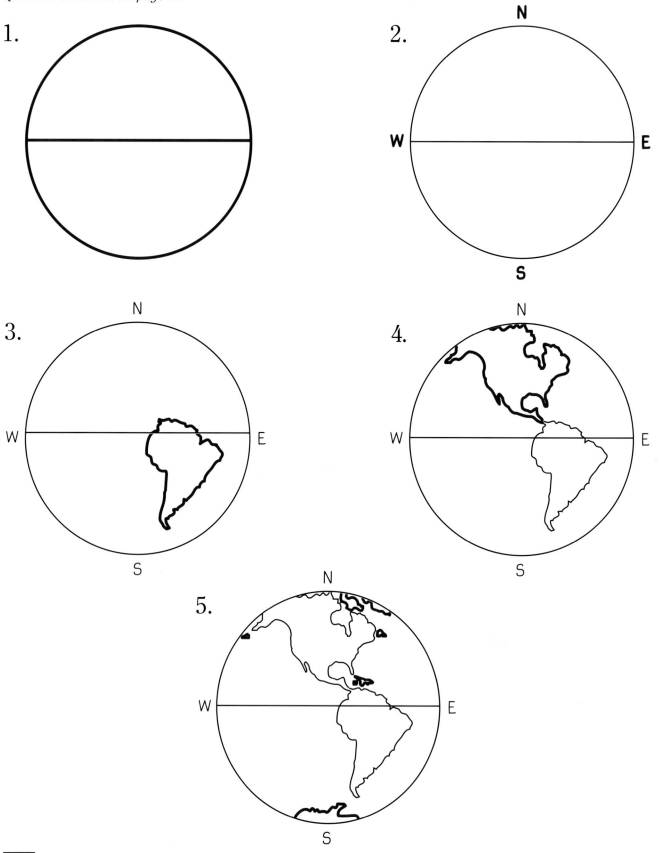

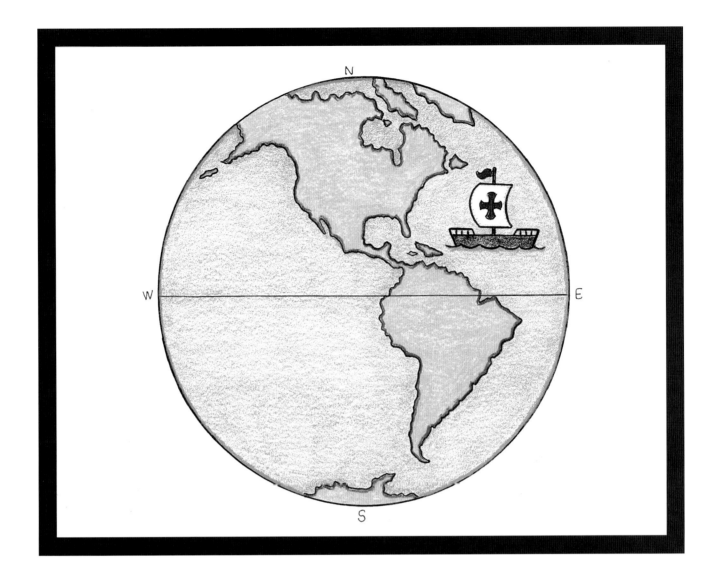

The world is round.
It is like a ball.
Columbus sailed west.
He wanted to sail to India.

What was missing from Columbus's map in 1492?

Europe

Africa

India

1492

Columbus had three ships.
Ninety men sailed on them.
They sailed for two months.
They landed on October 12.

How did Columbus find his way across the ocean?

The Niña, Pinta and Santa Maria

Teaching Tip on page 64
Question answered on page 22

1.

2.

3.

4.

5.

6.

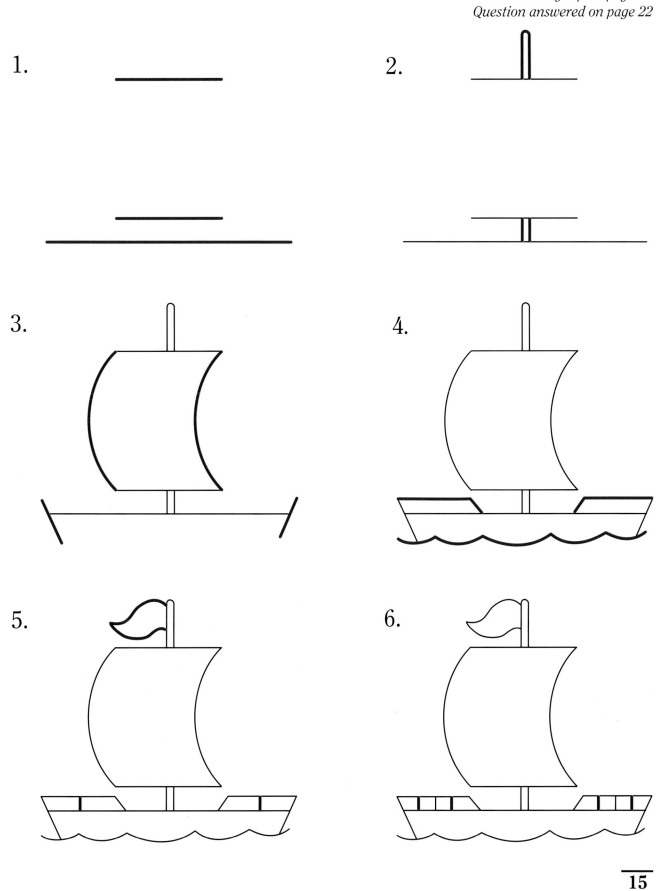

Reaching Land

Question answered on page 22

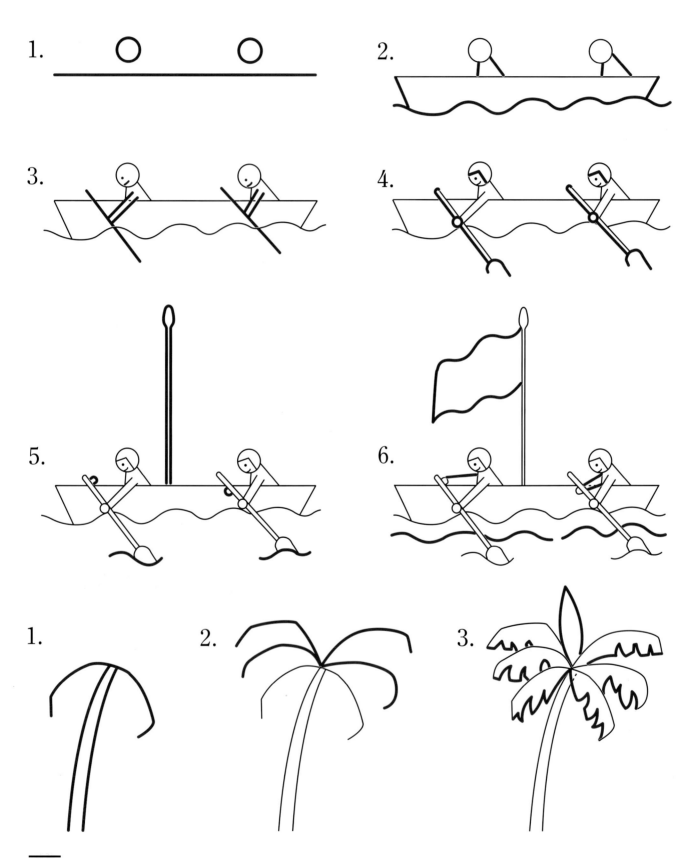

1.

2.

3.

4.

5.

6.

1.

2.

3.

Columbus landed in the Bahamas.
He claimed the land for Spain.
He thought he was near India.
He was in America.

How did Columbus's trip affect Europe?

There were people in America.
Columbus called them Indians.
They were good farmers.
They traveled in canoes.

How did Columbus's trip affect America?

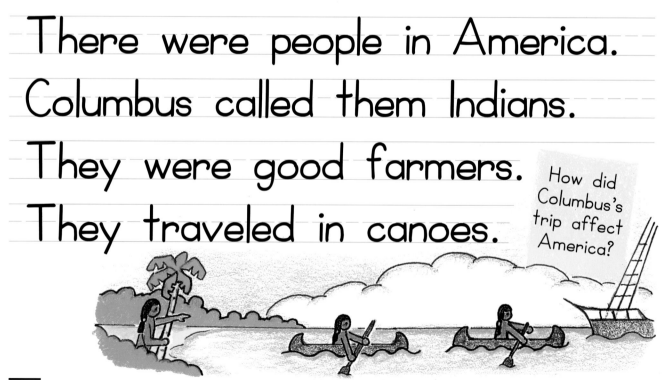

Question answered on page 22

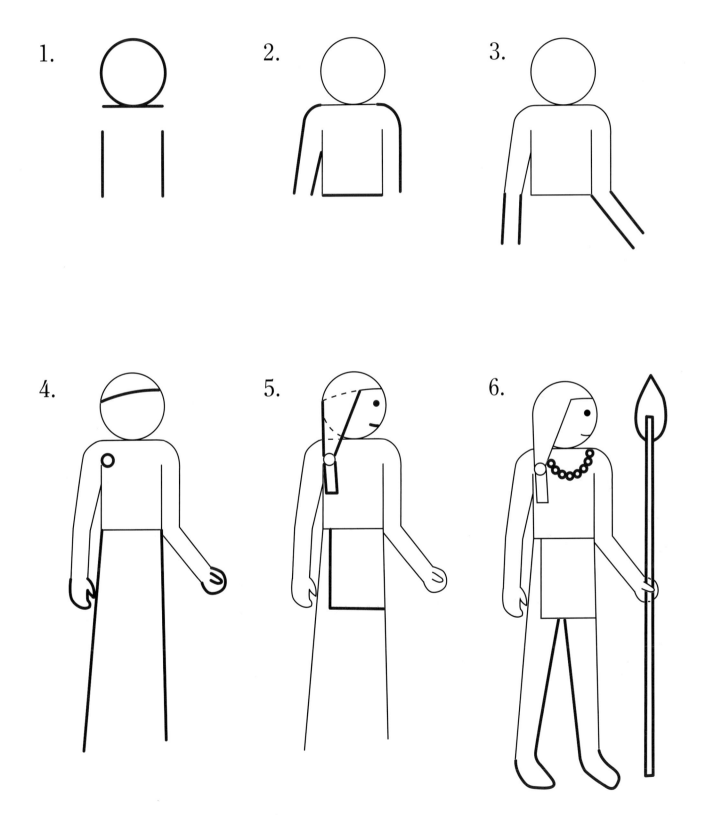

1.

2.

3.

4.

5.

6.

Draw What You See

Do you see the simple shapes used to draw people?

Circles for heads and hands?

Dots for eyes and lines for mouths?

Rectangles for bodies, arms and legs?

Do you want to add more details to your drawings?

Look at hands.

(page 10)

(page 18)

Your Hands!

Look at your face
in a mirror...

How would you draw
your eyes and mouth?

How would you draw
your nose?

Remember to place the eyes
in the middle of the head.

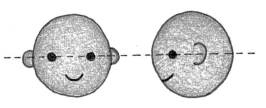

Learn more about Columbus...

BOOKS—AN IMPORTANT PART OF EXPLORATION!

Did Columbus trust his sailors? How did Columbus feel when he reached land? Today, people know his thoughts because he wrote them in a book. The book is called, I, COLUMBUS: MY JOURNAL 1492-1493 *edited by Peter and Connie Roop, illustrated by Peter E. Hanson, published by Avon Books, 1990.*

Columbus read a book—written 200 years earlier—about a man who traveled to China and India over land. The man's tales motivated Columbus to find a way to sail to the East Indies. Read about the explorer whose travels inspired Columbus in MARCO POLO *by Kathy Reynolds, illustrated by Daniel Woods, published by Raintree Steck-Vaughn, 1986.*

EXPLORATION CHANGES THE WAY WE SEE OUR WORLD

The Phoenicians, Mary Kingsley and Neil Armstrong were explorers. Read about these and other adventurous people in THE EXPLORER THROUGH HISTORY *by Julia Waterlow, illustrated by Tony Smith, published by Thomson Learning, 1994.*

A tribe thought they were the only people in the world until one of their members went exploring. Read ONE SMALL BLUE BEAD *by Byrd Baylor Schwitzer, illustrated by Ronald Himler, published by Macmillan, 1992.*

What's outside in the dark? A family goes on nighttime explorations in WALK WHEN THE MOON IS FULL *by Frances Hamerstrom, illustrated by Robert Katona, published by Crossing Press, 1975.*

Explore a make-believe island with talking animals in MY FATHER'S DRAGON *by Ruth Stiles Gannett, illustrated by Ruth Chrisman Gannett, published by Knopf, 1948.*

Autumn Harvest

Apples grow on trees.
They grow all summer long.
They get ripe in the fall.
Then we pick them.

What does "harvest" mean?

Apples

Teaching Tip on page 64
Question answered on page 48

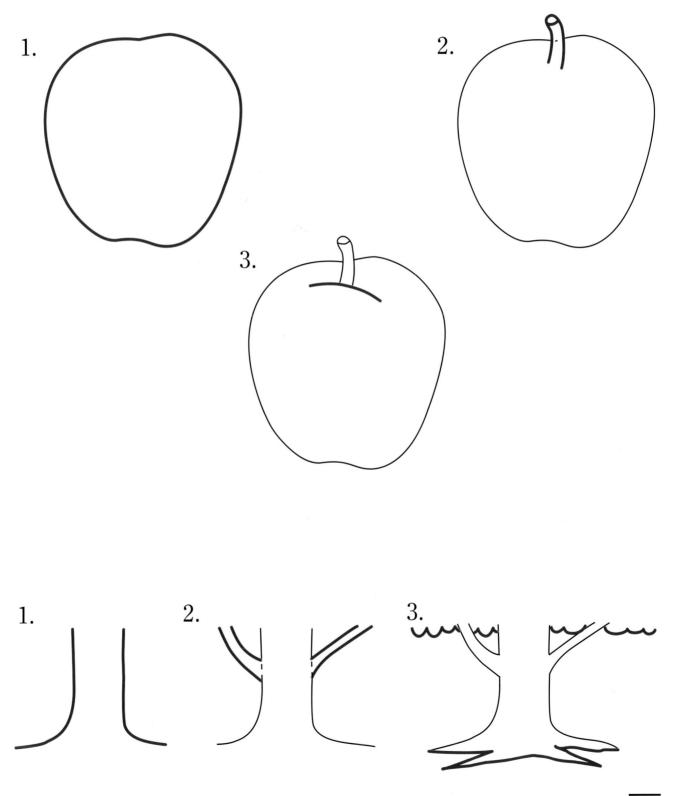

1.

2.

3.

1.   2.   3.

Grapes

Teaching Tip on page 64
Question answered on page 48

1.

2.

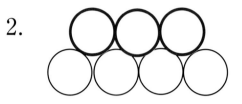

3.

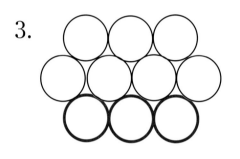

4.

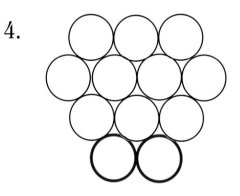

5.

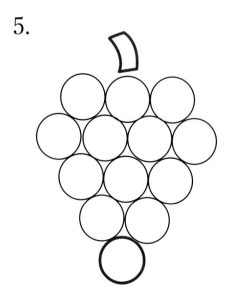

6.

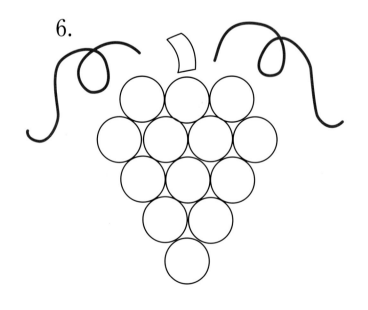

Grapes grow on vines.

They are juicy.

Sometimes they are dried.

Dried grapes are called raisins.

What is autumn?

Tree squirrels live in trees.
Ground squirrels live in burrows.
Both hunt for nuts and seeds.
They store food for winter.

What do squirrels do in the winter?

Teaching Tip on page 64
Question answered on page 48

Owl

Teaching Tip on page 64
Question answered on page 48

1.

2.

3.
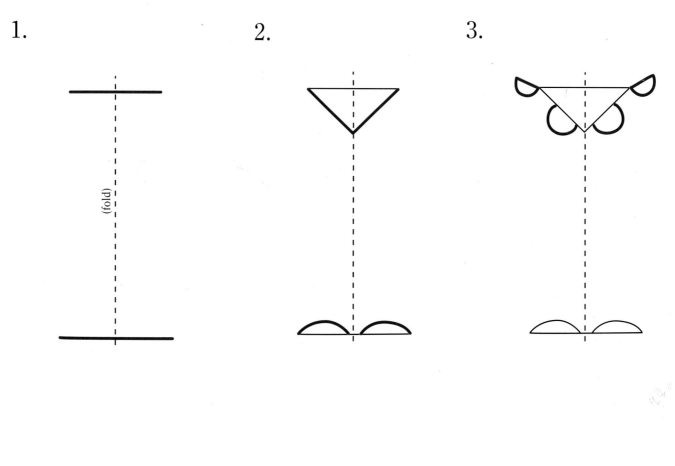

4.
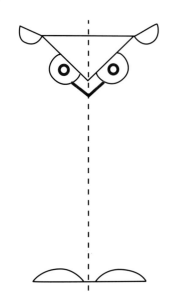

5.
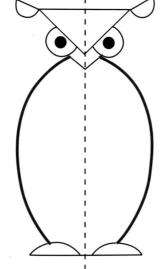

6.
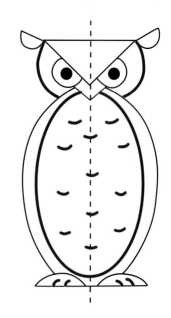

(fold)

Owls are awake at night.
They sit in trees.
Owls watch for food.
They see well in the dark.

Why are owls awake at night?

A flock of geese
Is flying along,
Southward for winter
Singing a song.

Author Unknown

Why do geese fly in the shape of a "V"?

1.

2.

3.

4.

5.

6.

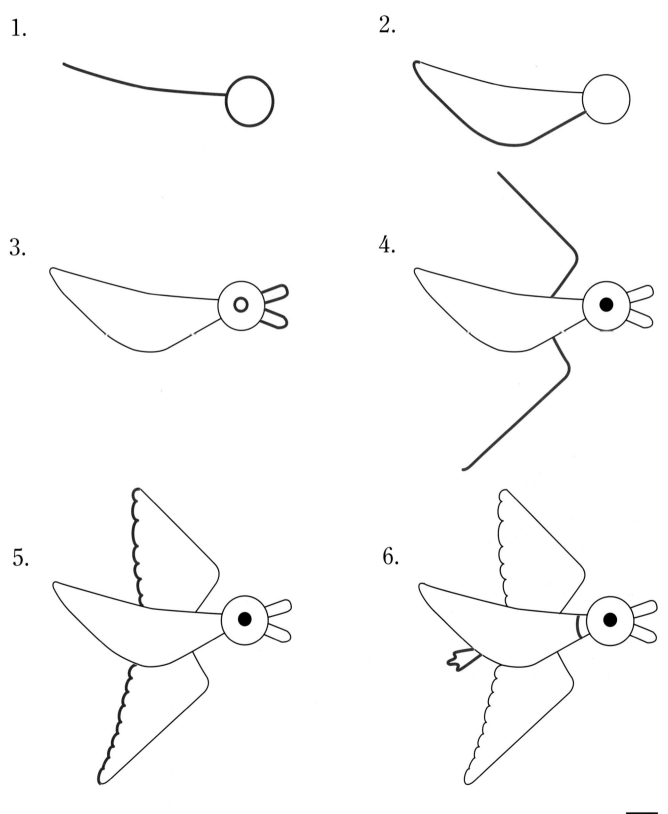

Pumpkin

Question answered on page 48

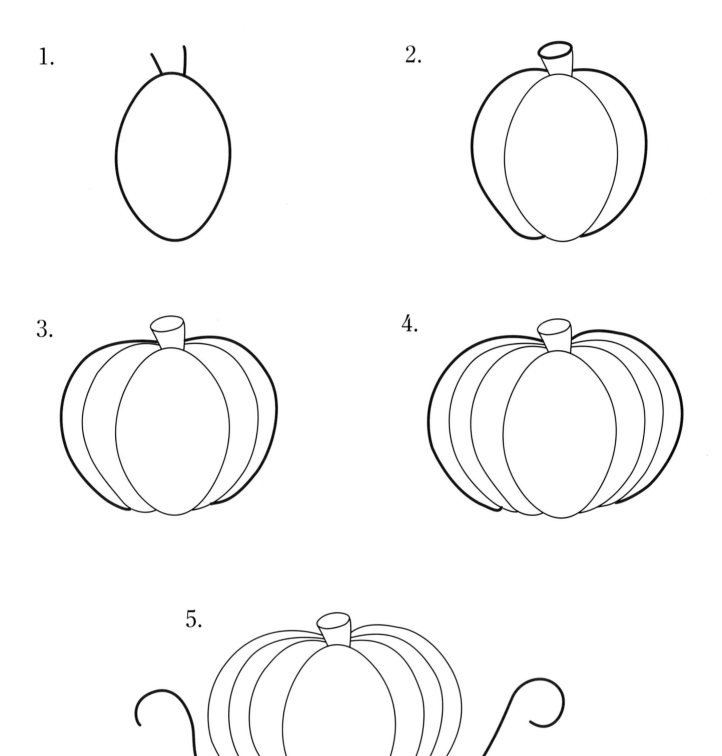

1.

2.

3.

4.

5.

Pumpkins grow on vines.
We pick them in the fall.
They are orange.
They make good pies.

What are some other orange things you see?

A scarecrow is in the field.
Will it scare the crows?
A farmer had fun making it.
He used his old clothes.

Why do farmers want to scare crows?

Scarecrow

Question answered on page 48

1.

2.

3.

4.

5.

6.

Deciduous Tree

Teaching Tip on page 64
Question answered on page 48

1.

2.

3.

4.

5.

6.

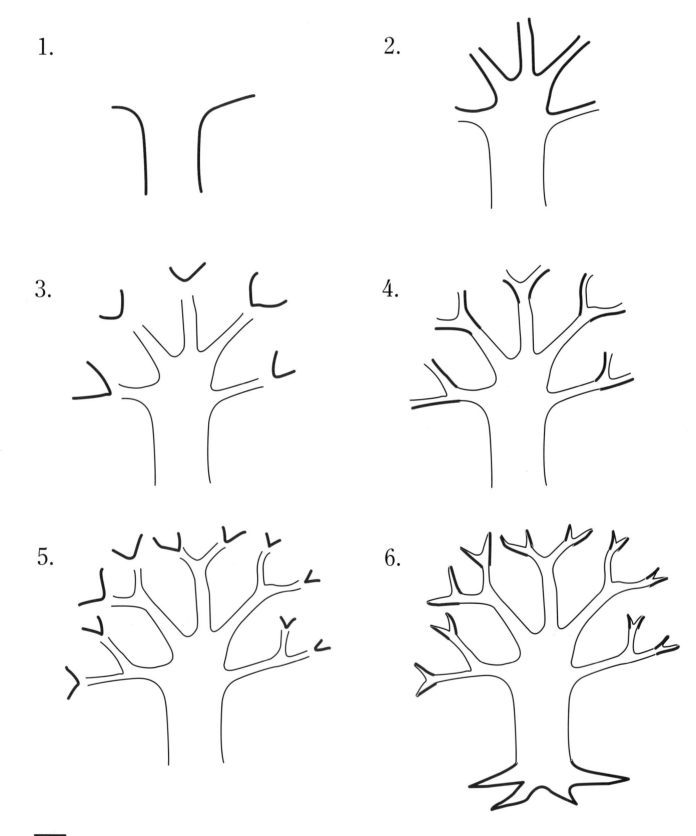

Some trees lose their leaves.
The leaves fall in autumn.
Branches are bare in winter.
New leaves grow in spring.

Are seasons the same all over the world?

Leaves make food for trees.
They make food all summer.
Leaves change in autumn.
They turn bright colors.

How long
do
trees live?

Leaves and Seeds

Question answered on page 48

Maple

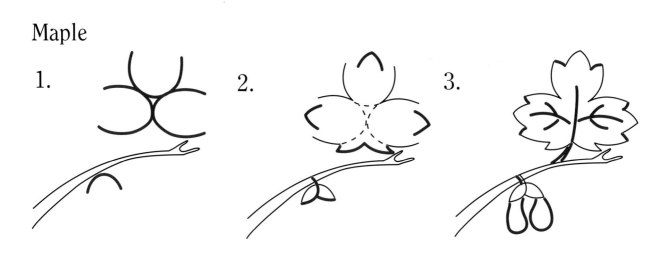

1.　　2.　　3.

Oak

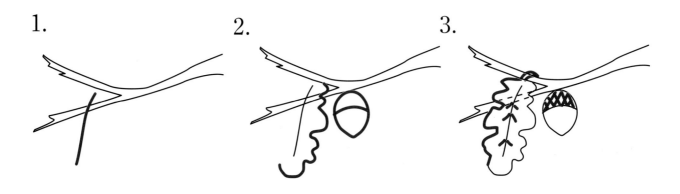

1.　　2.　　3.

Poplar

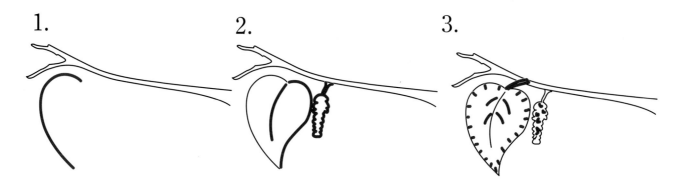

1.　　2.　　3.

Evergreen Tree

Question answered on page 48

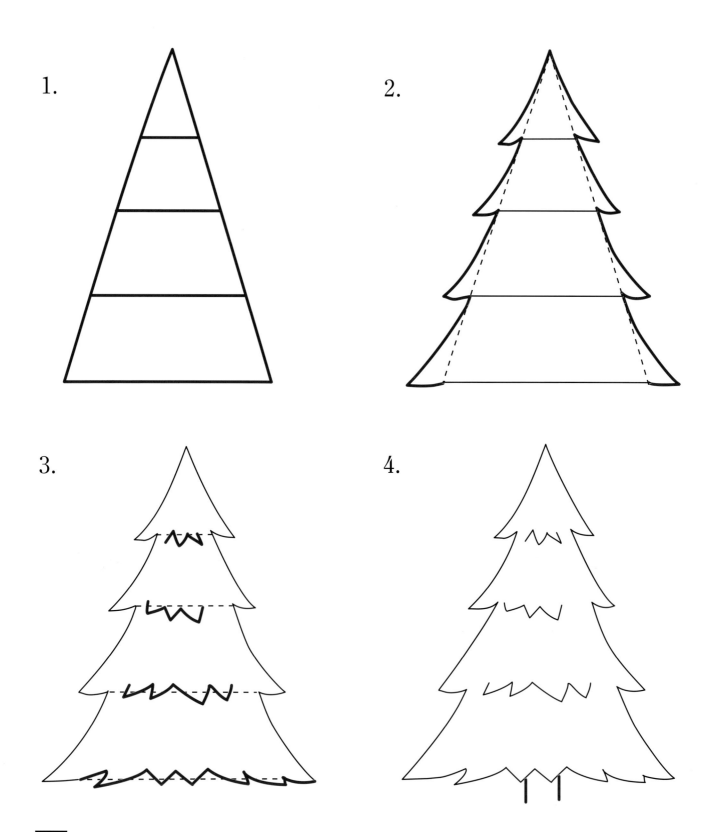

1.

2.

3.

4.

Evergreens stay green all year.
Their branches are never bare.
They drop their needles.
They lose a few at a time.

What lives in evergreen forests?

Some evergreens have needles.
Needles are their leaves.

Some evergreens have cones.
Seeds are in the cones.

How can you tell a pine tree from a fir tree?

Needles and Cones

Teaching Tip on page 64
Question answered on page 48

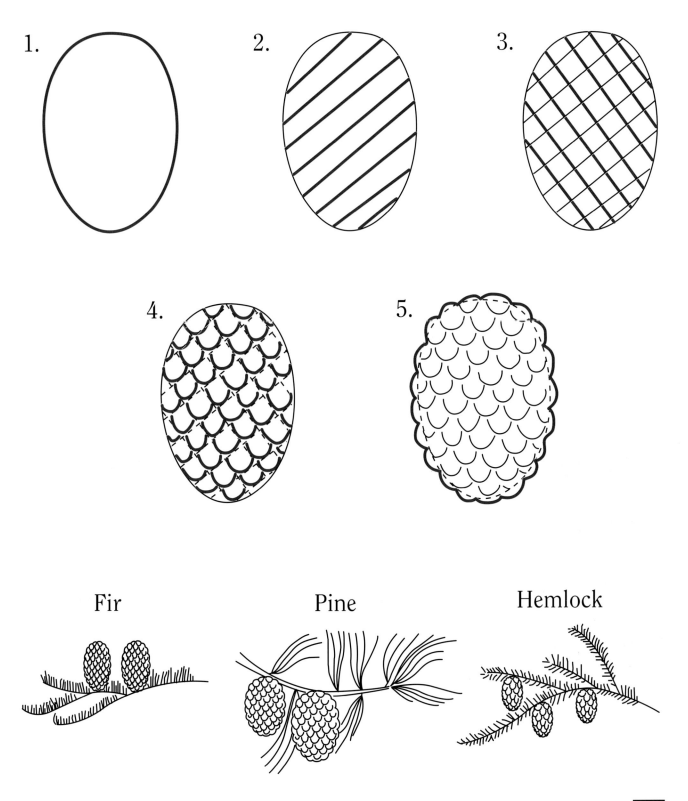

1.

2.

3.

4.

5.

Fir

Pine

Hemlock

Draw Your World

Where can you find repeated shapes and lines?

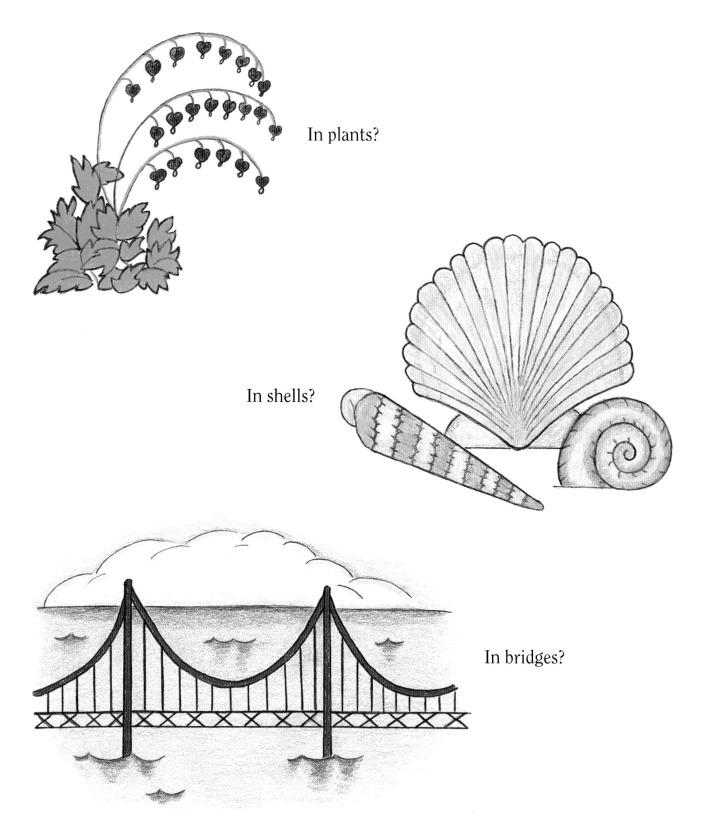

In plants?

In shells?

In bridges?

Can you design a border pattern?

Choose two shapes or lines from your drawing...

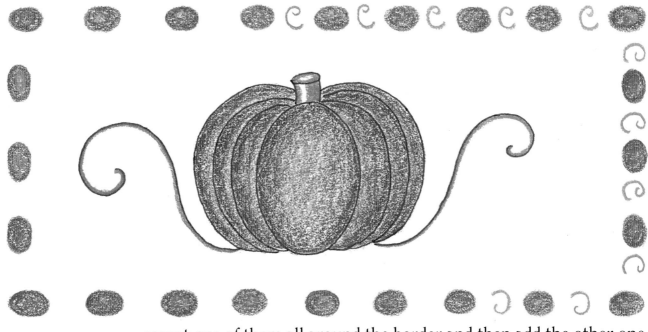

...repeat one of them all around the border and then add the other one.

(see more border patterns on pages 27, 35 and 39)

Do these drawings look the same on both sides?

When shapes and lines are repeated in a drawing to create a mirror image, it is called a symmetrical design.

(page 31)

(page 36)

(page 40)

On this side, the scarecrow has half a hat, half a face, one arm and one leg. | What does he have on this side of the line?

Learn more about harvest time...

The Weather

Tiny water drops make clouds.
They come from lakes and seas.
The drops are too small to see.
They rise into the sky.

How do tiny water drops rise into the sky?

Plane in the Clouds

Question answered on page 62

1.

2.

3.

4.

5.

6.

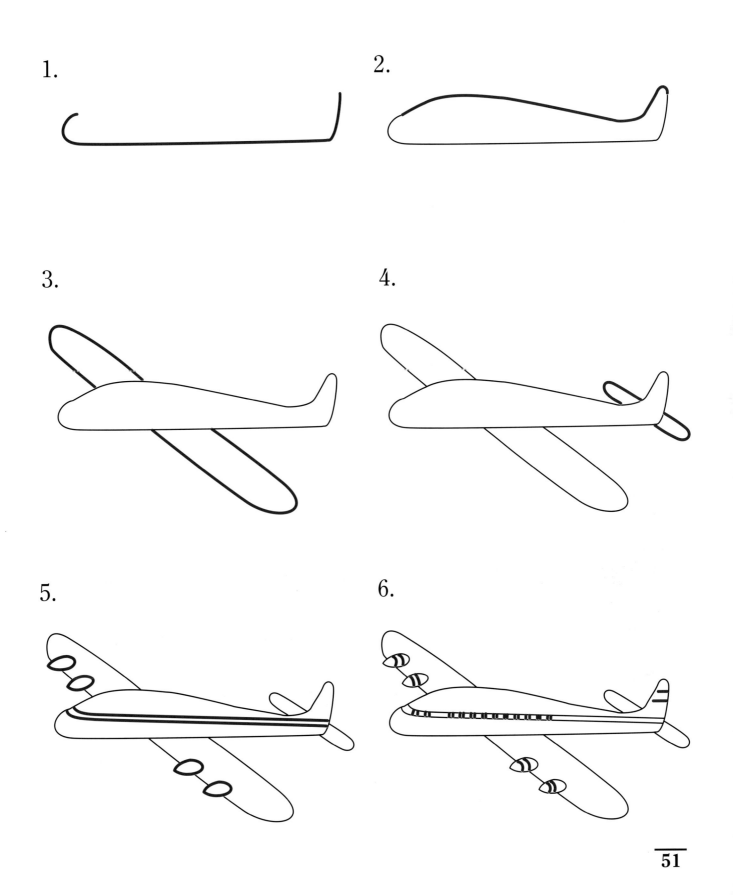

Truck in the Rain

Question answered on page 62

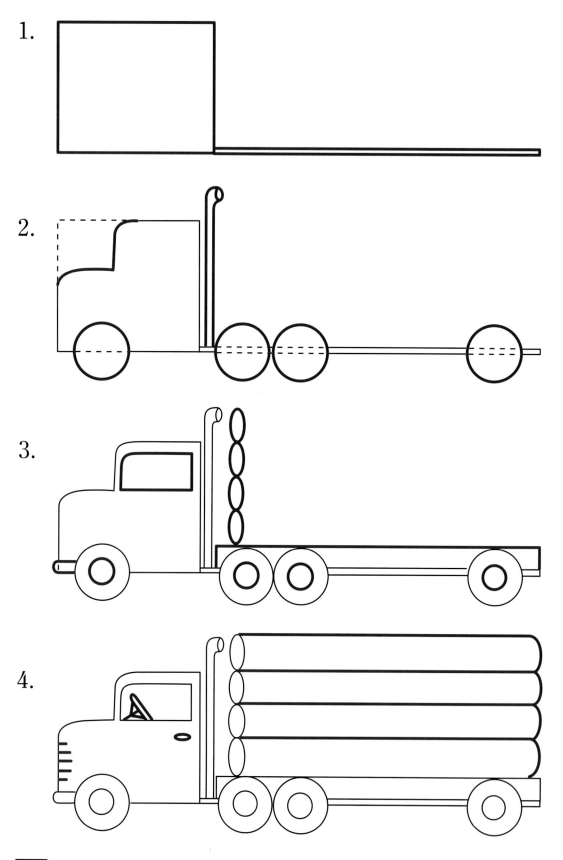

1.

2.

3.

4.

Sometimes a cloud is cooled.
The tiny drops come together.
They form raindrops.
The raindrops fall to earth.

Where does rain go after it has fallen to earth?

Some clouds get very cold.
The tiny drops freeze.
They form snowflakes.
The snowflakes fall to earth.

Why doesn't it snow in some places?

Sledding in the Snow

Teaching Tip on page 64
Question answered on page 62

1.

2.

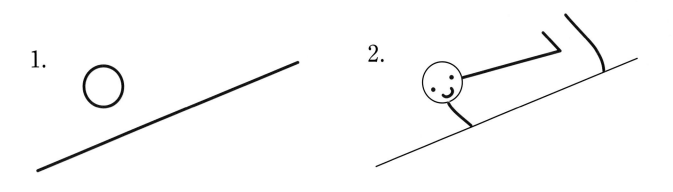

3.

4.

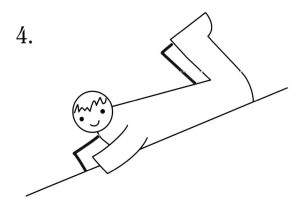

5.

6.

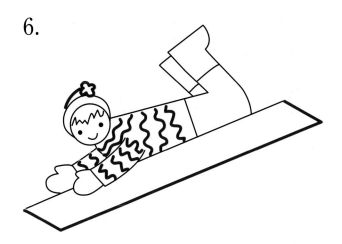

Car in the Fog

Question answered on page 62

1.

2.

3.

4.

5.

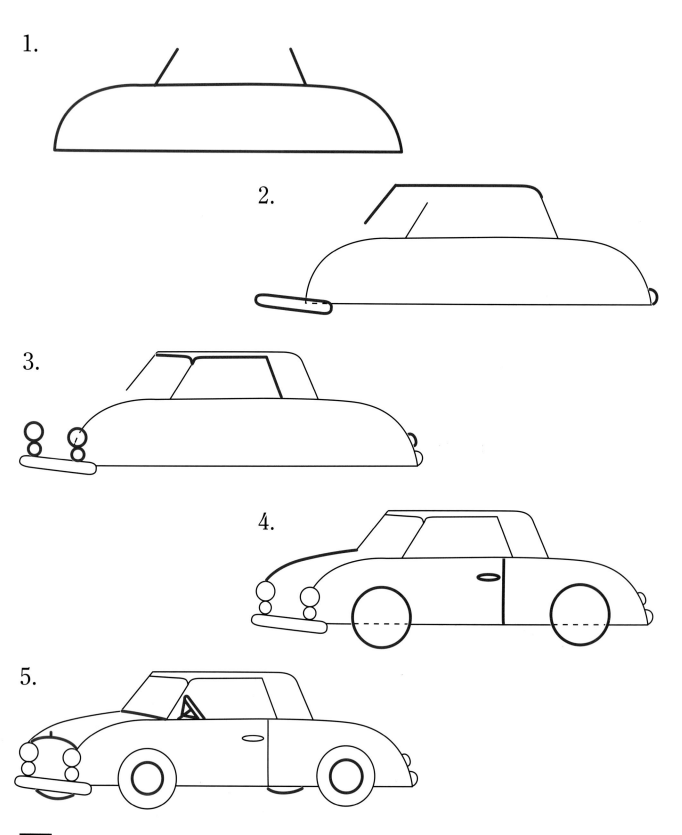

Fog is a cloud near the ground.
Fog feels cool and moist.
It is hard to see far in fog.
We drive carefully in fog.

Why are fog clouds close to the ground?

Wind pushes clouds.
It moves sailboats, too.
Wind can be strong.
Wind can be a gentle breeze.

How can wind be helpful? How can wind be harmful?

Sailboat in the Wind

Teaching Tip on page 64
Question answered on page 62

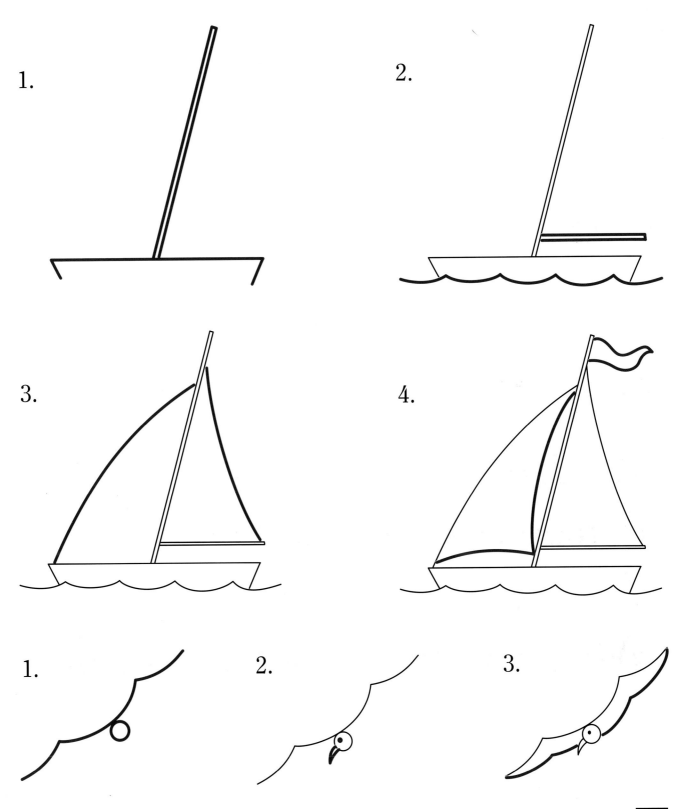

1.

2.

3.

4.

1.

2.

3.

Draw From Your Imagination

Can you imagine the subject you want to draw?

The subject is the main person or thing in your picture.
What size will it be?

Large?

Small?

Where will you draw the subject on the paper?

In the middle?

Near the bottom?

Near the top?

Can you imagine the background you want to draw?

The background shows where your subject is located.
Where would you draw a car?

In the woods?

In a race?

In a service station?

Will you add details to your drawing?

Details are the extra things you add to the subject and the background.
How many details will you add?

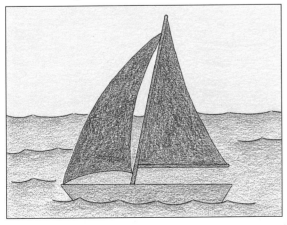

Few?

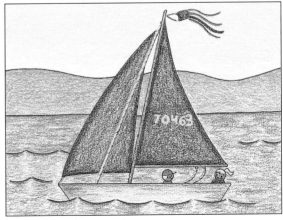

Many ?

Learn more about the weather...

How do tiny water drops rise into the sky?
Page 50

The sun warms the water in lakes, rivers and seas. Whenever water is warmed, tiny bits of it become an invisible gas. In this form, water is called vapor. See the changes in WATER'S WAY by Lisa Westberg Peters, illustrated by Ted Rand, published by Arcade, 1991.

Where does rain go after it has fallen to earth?
Page 53

Some of it soaks into the ground, collects in ponds or is used by living things. Most rain water flows downstream on a long trip to the ocean. Read FOLLOW THE WATER FROM BROOK TO OCEAN written and illustrated by Arthur Dorros, published by HarperCollins, 1991.

Why doesn't it snow in some places?
Page 54

Some places don't get cold enough for snow to form. Read TEMPERATURE AND YOU by Betsy Maestro, illustrated by Giulio Maestro, published by Lodestar Books, 1990.

Why are fog clouds close to the ground?
Page 57

Fog is a new cloud that forms when the ground is cooler than the air. It stays until the ground warms or the air cools. Fog can form quickly over land or water, as in LOST IN THE FOG by Irving Bacheller, adapted and illustrated by Loretta Krupinski, published by Little, Brown & Co., 1990.

How can wind be helpful? How can wind be harmful?
Page 58

In Whoopee, Wyoming, the wind was so strong it pulled feathers off chickens and tossed dogs into the air. A cowboy got so mad at the wind that he tried to get rid of it! Instead, he found the wind could help him. See how the wind was both helpful and harmful in JACK AND THE WHOOPEE WIND by Mary Calhoun, illustrated by Dick Gackenbach, published by W. Morrow, 1987.

Predicting weather—what will the weather be today?

Scientists use special equipment to predict the weather. Visit a weather station in WEATHER FORECASTING written and illustrated by Gail Gibbons, published by Four Winds Press, 1987.

Start your own weather station! Make a thermometer, weather vane, barometer and rain gauge with the help of WEATHER AND CLIMATE by Barbara Taylor, published by Kingfisher Books, 1993. Why are deserts found in some parts of the world, rain forests in others? How does the sun create wind on the earth?

Watch a groundhog on February 2 to predict the weather. Learn about this silly, special day in WHAT HAPPENED TODAY, FREDDY GROUNDHOG? written and illustrated by Marvin Glass, published by Crown, 1989.

Weather changes

See how weather changes in a powerful way in THE BIG STORM written and illustrated by Bruce Hiscock, published by Macmillan, 1993. In this book, the author follows a storm that crossed the United States in 1982.

What if, instead of rain, french fries fell from clouds? Appetizing weather prevails in the tall tale CLOUDY WITH A CHANCE OF MEATBALLS by Judi Barrett, illustrated by Ron Barrett, published by Macmillan, 1978.

Teaching Tips

Christopher Columbus

SAILING WEST (page 12) — Point out that North America is centered in the northern hemisphere and South America is mostly in the southeast quarter. The mouth of the Amazon River is at the equator. Don't expect the children to draw every detail.

by Michelle Stitzer, age 8

THE NIÑA, PINTA AND SANTA MARIA (page 15) — Describe the cross shown on the sail on page 14 as a big "+" sign with fat ends. The children may prefer to add it during coloring time. Use a red crayon, color pencil or marker to make a large "+" sign, fatten it, then finish by widening the ends.

Autumn Harvest

APPLES (page 25) — Demonstrate how shiny, smooth surfaces like a glazed ceramic vase reflect light and appear white (or lighter in color) on the curved surface. Note how the apples are colored so they look as if they are reflecting light.

GRAPES (page 26) — Explain to the children that the circles in this drawing are all the same size. You may want to draw horizontal guidelines for younger children.

SQUIRREL (page 29) — Describe the body and head as a big number "3" (step 1). The ears are a number "3" tipped on its side (step 2).

Symmetrical   Asymmetrical

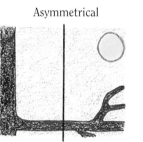

OWL (page 30) — Create the center guideline by folding the paper in half (step 1). The owl is a symmetrical design—the drawing on the left side of the center guideline is the same as the right side. The background drawing of the tree and moon is an asymmetrical design—different lines and shapes are drawn on each side of the center guideline and yet they balance visually.

DECIDUOUS TREES (page 38) — Branches start with a V-shape (steps 2, 3 and 5). New branches are thinner (steps 4 and 6).

NEEDLES AND CONES (page 45) — Show the children a pineapple. Note that the diagonal pattern on a pineapple is similar to the pattern on cones. When a pineapple is sitting upright, its scales look like upside down "U's". What direction do the "U's" on a pinecone point?

The Weather

SLEDDING IN THE SNOW (page 55) — The snowman and sledders are all subjects in this picture. Point out that there can be more than one subject in a picture, just as there can be more than one character in a story.

SAILBOAT IN THE WIND (page 59) — Challenge the children to draw the gull in the foreground of the picture on page 58. Can they do it without step-by-step instructions?